D1236829

Come On, Let's Pray!

Prayers for Personal and Family Worship

Compiled by
VIRGINIA LAW

Edited by
RONALD PATTERSON

FOREWORD

If the story could be told, what a thrilling record it would be—the extensive influence and vitality released through families praying together!

If the cynics, who mouth their unrealistic doubts about the worth and lasting value of the family, could only see what strong contributions prayer has made to the advancement of human living!

Within these pages are recorded a wide range and diversity of helpful prayers—etched in words, nurtured in hearts, dreamed in minds. Some of these were first spoken in the quiet inner life; others have been spoken in the corporateness of family groupings.

These are prayers which will abide, helpful to many, useful to adults and youth, cherished by women and men—anywhere and any time.

The Upper Room gladly shares this compilation with the hope that all readers will derive lasting benefit.

Wilson O. Weldon, Editor
The Upper Room

Contents

Chapter 9. Morning and Evening Prayers

Evening

Morning

CHAPTER 1

Prayers of Gratitude and Thanksgiving

Our Thanksgiving

Dear God, Father of creation and bounty, of life and love, we have no way to repay you for bringing us into being, directing your love toward us, and being always mindful of our needs. You not only know that we cannot repay you, but also that you do not expect it; for we and all things are yours from the beginning to the end.

As for us, we know it is not your design that we be insensitive as cold stones or accept food and drink, as do beasts, without any sense of gratitude. You have created us in your image—not like stone,

9

but capable of feeling; not mere animals acting on instinct, but capable of intelligent action based on thinking back and thinking ahead; not without knowledge of you, but aware of you and your supremacy and therefore we can thank and praise and worship you.

- You think of us—
  Help us to think often of you.
- You act in our behalf—
  Help us to act with your will in mind.
- You have love for us—
  Help us to respond in love for you.
- You have appreciation for our lives—
  Help us to use our potentials to your glory.

So may we express in token fashion our joy for the life you give us while sustaining us with your blessings daily and without number. Amen.

—Russell Q. Chilcote

The Cricket
The cricket chirps.
It makes music unto the Lord.
It sings never ending praises
For the glory of God.
Lord, make me a cricket.
Let me sing endlessly songs of praise.
Praise of your Son, Jesus Christ.
Praise for the wonderful life inside me.
Praise of your never ending love.
Praise of your glory.
Amen.

—David Randolph III

Thank You, Lord

It's me again, Lord, wanting to talk. I just have to thank you again for your goodness to me. You truly are great, and I praise and adore your name.

Thank you for my life's partner, and for the happiness I enjoy because of his devotion. Thank you for the gift of children to delight and inspire our home. Thank you for friends who know you so well, and for the beautiful oneness we share because of you. Thank you for opportunities and experiences in living that challenge and help me grow.

And most of all, I thank you for your marvelous love that is so real I feel it. Thank you for the joy you give when I yield my being to be filled with your Spirit. My cup is running over. Thank you for the peace you grant when I walk by faith. For all that I seek and need, you do so freely give. Thank you, God, that in companionship with you, I find the answers to the complexities of life. Amen.

—Marilyn Tarrant

Gratitude for the Church

Almighty God, the Father of all people, I come before thee with praise and thanksgiving. I have so much to be thankful for and I remember thy promise that whatever we ask, believing with faith, we shall receive.

I give thee thanks for letting me be a part of the church that I might give of my time and gifts to the on-going of thy kingdom.

May we always be thankful for the unending mercies and blessings which we recognize as coming from thee each day of our lives. While we hold many possessions in this world, keep us ever mindful that we hold them only as a trust.

Help us to be good stewards of thy great bounty. In Jesus' name we pray. Amen.

—Fleeta Davis

Turned On to the Spirit

Hey God,

The other night was really something. Do you remember when some people came over to our house and shared with us? We talked, sang, and prayed . . . But it was a rare experience because all of us were dropping our masks and being real with each other.

And do you know who we were talking and singing about? You! Later when we began to sing, there was a great movement among and within us. It was one of the highest, most significant, and deeply joyous movements of your Spirit that we have ever shared together.

Our very foundations were loosened and we were awakened and freed to participate in your love and joy. Indeed, we felt a shared sense of the sacredness of life, and it was beautiful! The old folks would say, "We felt the Spirit mov'n." The young would say we got "turned on" to your Spirit. Surely, both young and old are right, for in an imperfect way, we were moved (awed) and "turned on" to the reality and spirit of your love. Thank you, Jesus.

—Mark Eugene Fentress

Prayer of Thanks

Father, gratitude does not come easy to us. It's one thing to ask you to give us something, but it's much more difficult to face the fact that you have already given us more than we deserve. What can we do, but in our moments of honesty, humbly blurt out those hard words—"Thank you."

Thank you for **progress.** It would be nice if we could take credit for our technological achievement and industrial genius. But truthfulness calls us to the awareness that you are the breath of life, and what we accomplish comes as a result of our sensitive and effective use of the talent and ability you have given. What more can we say than, "Thank you."

Thank you for **freedom.** It would be hell to live a puppet existence—boxed in by some predetermined plan in which we had no freedom to choose or decide. If you make one thing clear in the life and ministry of Jesus, it is that we are called to be decisive and, yes, even responsible persons. What more can we say than, "Thank you."

Thank you for **love.** So often we have been caught up in our own self-interests, still you patiently wait and accept us back when we come to our senses. We have been nonchalant, even apathetic about the needs that surround us, yet you remain responsive to our hurts and defeats. We talk about love, plastering it on banners, wearing it on jewelry, even singing it in our songs, but by your love we are changed from harlotry into new persons. What more can we say than, "Thank you."

Thank you for **power.** We all need to feel as if what we do is worthwhile. You promised, "You will be filled with power when the Holy Spirit comes on you." That in itself gives us hope. We are your pilgrim people, blazing a new frontier each day, receiving and using the power which you offer. No wonder we cry out with gratitude and thanksgiving, "This is the day which the Lord has made, let us rejoice and be glad in it."

—Robert Ochsenrider

For God's Goodness

Thank you, God:

That we are fortunate enough to live in a country where we are able to live and worship as we choose. . . .

That we are able to see your beautiful world, to work, and play in it. . . .

That we have food, warm homes, and lovely possessions to delight and satisfy. . . .

That you have given us families and friends, doctors and medicines, books and music—necessities and extras we take for granted while others hold them priceless. . . .

So, Lord, we pray:

For forgiveness, because we waste so much and complain that we do not have more. . . .

For more sensitivity to our neighbors' loneliness and frustrations, more understanding of their differences and dreams. . . .

For help to praise you more; to know your Son and his ways more perfectly, so that we may live more unselfishly, thoughtfully, and serve more compassionately—that others may know we are Christians by our love. Amen.

—Mary Ann Hunt

Thanks for Life
Father, we thank you for life;
simple, yet complex; joyful, yet sad;
at times dull, or filled with pain;
at times brimming over with gaiety and hope.
We thank you, Father, for life,
rooted and grounded in love.
For love comprehends, and goes beyond
joy and pain, hope and fear.
Love is at the heart of all life,
if we would but look and see.

We thank you for your gift of creativity,
of love taking on shape,
of prayer and tears, happiness and sorrow,
somehow poured into the forms
and colors and textures of loveliness.
For the sharing we have with you
in forming and fashioning life.
For all of this,
we thank you, Lord.
Amen.

—J. Barrie Shepherd

CHAPTER 2

Prayers for Christian Living

For Christ's Presence

Father, we thank you for all that has happened in our lives since we put our trust in your Son and have sought to follow him. May we be "teachable" and aware of our Christian witness in all of life.

May we be aware that many people want to see a "working model" of a Christian before they make their own decision. May our home be a haven of rest for those with questions and problems. May your love so flow through our actions and reactions that people will know we belong to you. In Jesus' name. Amen.

—Harbert Thornton

Victorious Life

Our heavenly Father, our life vanishes as the morning dew in the bright noonday sun. Yet we learn that through thy wonderful providence thou hast put mysterious power into our short life, giving us a task to fulfill before we reach the end of our life on earth.

We pray thou wilt be merciful and strengthen us who wander in the perplexity and dismay of this world. Though we be at the place of winter's chilling wind, or icy bleak place, guide us to see the hope of thy eternal kingdom.

Thou who art our great and loving Shepherd, who seeks one stray sheep, leaving behind ninety-nine others, help us who stray as lost sheep and lead us into thy fold.

Guide us to walk the way of victory, trusting in eternal glory, and serving thee to the end. And even when we face death, grant us to look up to thy eternal kingdom without fear.

In the name of our Lord Jesus Christ. Amen.

—Toyohiko Kagawa

A Man's Prayer

Dear heavenly Father,

In these busy days in which I live, I find it impossible to attend to even the most basic needs of my family, the people who depend on me at work, and to my responsibilities in the community in which I live.

And yet you, O God, so wonderfully provide not only for all of mankind, but even for the sparrows and the lilies of the field!

Please teach me, Father, how to so live in your love that I may fulfill my responsibilities as you would have me to do.

I pray in Jesus' name. Amen.

—Walt Yarbrough

Forgive and Give

Our dear heavenly Father, we praise thee for thy great love for us, thy children. We are thankful that thy dear Son taught us to know thee as Father. We praise thee for thy Father-love of forgiveness, of redemption, and of healing. Help us to live thy forgiving, redeeming, and healing love as shown to us by thy Son. Help us to forgive and to give as he forgave and gave.

As we have forgiven those who have sinned against us, forgive us for the sins we have committed against thy children who are our brothers and sisters. We pray that always Thou wilt find in our hearts thy forgiving, redeeming, and healing love for all thy children. We can pray that our love for thee and thy children will increase each day.

We make our prayer for the sake of thy Son, Jesus Christ our Lord. Amen.

—Harry Denman

For New Experiences

It's an exciting opportunity and challenge, Father. Thank you for allowing this new venture to come my way. I feel woefully inadequate and even frightened, but will trust you to help me. I thank you for past experiences in which you revealed the presence and guidance of the Holy Spirit in such a way that I knew it wasn't my wisdom, but yours.

I claim your promise of being with me always—that if I will obediently walk in faith with you—and prepare myself as best I can, that you will assume the responsibility of results. I ask, too, for grace sufficient to accept your results whatever they may be.

Thank you for not demanding success of me, but for asking only that I be faithful and obedient to your call. I dedicate and give all of myself to you, to be used for your glory. Thank you for using me as you see fit. Amen.

—Ron Tarrant

For Daily Living

Dear Father, thank you for the challenges of this new day. Help me to realize that today can be either a stumbling block or a stepping stone depending upon how I use it, and how I give you the opportunity to move in my life.

The business world is so often a brutal world, but so was the world that crucified your Son. Let me open my heart to those principles of life which he would have me follow. Let me realize that the only way the world can really be changed, is for Christians to be used by your Holy Spirit. Help me to be willing to be one of those people. If I am not, I am wasting both your time and mine chasing rainbows. Help me to be open, available, and perceptive to the touch of your Spirit. Amen.

—William E. Robertson

A Clean Heart

O God, I thank you that you are my Father, and that I can spend this day in your presence. Thank you for your guidance, and the assurance of your provision.

How I praise you that Jesus is my Savior, and that he died for me. Show me those sins yet unknown to me, that I may confess them to you and know more of your cleansing power.

Create within me a clean heart that I may be filled with your Holy Spirit. Help me to be your person in my home and with my friends that I might be used for your purposes.

I commit myself to you today, Lord, trusting you to work out all things, that your glory might be seen in my life. In Jesus' name. Amen.

—Marion Millett

To Follow the Prince of Peace

Our loving Father, we know that peace is your wish for us, for You sent Jesus, the Prince of Peace, to show us the way.

Forgive us for turning from that way of peace. Too often we forget the soft answer and use the grievous words that stir up anger.

Peace is your gift to us, held out for us to take in prayer, in learning about our Savior and the path he trod. Yet again and again we spurn your gift, preferring to go our own willful way. O Father, we thank you for your love and patience, for never withholding from us the gift of peace. We may refuse a thousand times to take it, but it is always there for us to accept.

Father, help us in our family to strive for peace, thus lighting one small candle which may illumine those around us. Amen.

—Mrs. Alan Walker

Commitment

O God, your love is steadfast.
You stick with us through thick and thin,
but we unglue ourselves from you.
Call us back now, that we may respond
to your constant love
with unyielding loyalty.
Through Jesus Christ, who never lets go.
Amen.

—Richard P. Mathison

CHAPTER 3

Prayers for Times of Crisis

When Disappointment Comes

Dear heavenly Father, at times it is hard for us to understand why things happen as they do; our hearts grow heavy when our hopes and dreams are broken. Help us to know that thou art the same yesterday, today, and forever, and dost work in all things for our good. Teach us patience, lest we be swept away by the disappointment of the moment and become bitter or resentful. May this experience draw us closer to one another and to thee, so that when the night of disappointment has passed, we may rejoice in the day of gladness, fairer than we had ever dreamed. For Jesus' sake. Amen.

—William B. Oglesby, Jr.

In Time of Sorrow

O God, where are you? My world suddenly has lost all meaning. As I stood there beside the grave I couldn't help asking, Lord, "What is the meaning of life? How can I live in a world without this one who has been my very life?"

I know so little about you. But I dare to make one earnest plea—that this dear one has not died in vain. Help me even in my sorrow to discover the real meaning of life.

Lord, I feel so empty. Yet I sense somehow that you can become my fullness. Fill me, while I cling to my faith in Jesus your son, in whose name I pray. Amen.

—Dean Albritton

When a Dear One Is Sick

Dear God, as I sit here in the hospital beside my loved one's bed, I pray for him and for the others here with him who are suffering—the old, the young, and even tiny babies. I hear prayers of, "Lord, have mercy on me," "Help me, please God," or wordless prayers which are shown only in their eyes. Do give them courage and faith, dear Father, and may the ministrations of doctors and nurses bring relief to their pain-racked bodies.

I pray also for those of us who are up and well. May we realize that we must not wait until we are ill to pray, but help us to be ever thankful for all good things. When sickness and suffering come, help us to see them through the eyes of faith. Amen.

—Mrs. Edward Dickerson

For Healing

O blessed Lord, who art closer than breathing, nearer than hands or feet, I come to thee for healing. Since thou hast made me, certainly thou canst remake me. Give me the faith and belief that I may feel thy healing hand upon me. Bless all those who minister to my needs. May they feel their dependence upon thee for thy wise direction and guidance. I place myself in thy care, and know that thy love will watch over me and those dear to my heart. In Jesus' name. Amen.

—Rudolph L. Samuelson

Despair

Dear Comforter,
We are a sad, disillusioned, troubled people,
burdened with anxiety, guilt, and fear
for our nation and our families. Never has our
need been greater. Never have we so needed
an awareness of your gift, the Comforter.

In the devastating loss of lives,
of values, and of relationships which war,
loss of faith, and moral confusion
have bequeathed us,
may we seek anew the Prince of Peace
who alone can restore our faith and unity.

Give us courage to change our direction
and our wills when we or our policies are wrong.
Lead us into truth,
wholeness of mind and spirit,
as we ask and receive the gift of the Comforter.

Take our sorrow,
and in compassion heal our despair
with your gift of new faith
which can lead us into unlimited opportunities.
In the name of Jesus. Amen.

—Loma Haines

Marital Crisis

O God, I discovered today that my mate is in love with someone else. Please help me; I feel like a crumbled clay pot. The darkness is so dark and my prayers are not rising above my head. I saw them look at each other today and saw the love in their eyes. You said you would not leave nor forsake us—nor give us more than we could stand. You promised to be with us, but where are you? Please help me to keep my eyes off circumstances and keep them on you. . . .

Today I saw the two of them together and it hurt me so. But I am grateful that you have given me the strength to bear it and, yes, to even love through it all. You said to love your enemies, to do good to them which hate you, to bless them that curse you and pray for them which despitefully use you. But if they only knew how much it hurts! Do you, Lord?

They told me today, Father, that a divorce is inevitable. Friends are taking sides, and the children are confused and bewildered. Give me the strength for the living of these days. I cannot face them alone. I ask this in the name of your Son, given to us out of your love. Amen.

—Anonymous

Loss of a Child

Dear Father, grief overwhelms me. My child is dead! But we are not alone. Your promised Holy Spirit came to comfort me the moment I fell on my knees and cried, "O God, O God!"

The Body of Christ is so real, Lord. Letters keep pouring in to assure us of prayers; neighbors bring food to sustain; and friends come to weep with us. Through these gestures we find the calm of your peace which passes human understanding.

Love surrounds us. We seem to experience a share of that new life our child has entered: free from the limitations of time and space, free always to think and work for those things which are true, honest, pure, love filled, and of good report.

How conscious we are of your love, Father; of you as our burden bearer; your victory over death. We praise you, we adore you, we glorify you. We who have sown in tears reap in joy, for we know of your love and are persuaded that you will keep the one we have committed to you this day. Amen.

—Loma Haines

CHAPTER 4

Prayers for School Life

On the First Day of School

Our Father, on this first day of school, as each of us goes to a new grade, a new teacher, and new work, help us to hold closely to thy hand in this adventure. Keep us thoughtful of others, obedient to authority, and alert to learn. Make it a happy day, a day in which we shall grow, even as Christ grew, in wisdom, in stature, and in favor with God and our fellow men. In his name we pray. Amen.

—Ethel Miller

Prayer for Teachers

Eternal God, we pray for the teachers in our schools. Enrich them with wisdom, love, patience, and kindness. May they take Jesus, the Master Teacher, as their example. May their illustrations be as simple as his parables so those things which seem difficult may be easily understood. May they be patient with their students who are slow to learn and challenge those who are quick. May their dedicated service impart strength to our nation and this troubled world. Guide them into truth we pray. Amen.

—Margaret Morgan Watts

A Parent's Prayer

Father, we love _____ very much. Thank you for giving him (her) to us during these most formative years to guide and teach. To leave him (her) now hurts very much, yet we wouldn't have it any other way. We trust him (her) into your care. We know that you're with him (her) today, just as much as you were yesterday when he (she) was still with us.

We ask that he (she) might always remember that which was good and right that we taught him (her). Enable him (her), by your Holy Spirit, in these coming days, to discern truth from error, the best from that which is good. Lead him (her) in due time to that vocation to which you would call, and to that someone with whom you would have him (her) share his (her) life.

Thank you very much for being our Father and for understanding so completely on a day like this.

Through Christ, your Son, we pray. Amen.

—Bob Stamps

Before Examinations

Dear God, examinations are a bad time for the whole family. We need your presence and your help.

We all get scared of failure. We get tense and rough in our relationships with each other. Help us through this time.

For those who take exams, we pray for a good feeling—calmness, confidence, quickness of mind and hand, that the exams may go well.

For the rest of us, help us to be sensitive to what's going on—the pressures, the doubts and fears. Teach us to be supporting and helpful, quiet or friendly, according to each moment's need.

You did command us to love you with all our minds. We will try. Give us wisdom and courage for this time of examination. Help us all to learn and practice the disciplines of study and preparation that we may be able to come through in all the great tests of life. In the name of Jesus Christ we pray. Amen.

—Jameson Jones

A Student's Prayer on the First Day of College

God, this is a big day for me. It's great to know you lead the way here, that you were here before me and have come here with me.

I come to this day with mixed emotions: sad yet happy, afraid yet expectant. Thank you for all the good things and good people that you have used to shape my life thus far. I commit all those that I love to your care. Teach me, even though right now I would rather go back, not to be afraid of a change in the course of my life. Give me courage to follow you.

We've come this far together and I intend to follow you for the rest of my life. I thank you that I don't need to be afraid of truth. I commit my mind and my body, my will and heart to you anew today at this great new beginning. I acknowledge you as the Living Truth. I will honor you through these years of my formal education as Lord of all creation, Lord of history, and Lord of my own heart.

Help me to be sensitive today to the needs of those around me. Enable me to be a friend and to make the right friends. May I always avail myself of every opportunity to share the new life I have found in Christ with those who are seeking you.

Lead on Master! Amen!

—Bob Stamps

CHAPTER 5

Prayers for Family Relationships

Prayer for Husbands and Wives

Almighty God, who has put the solitary in families, who has made us to be lovers of the world and of each other, we thank you for all quickening of life, all delights of touch and closeness, all pleasures of eye and ear and common desire, which make it so splendid to be human. May we not take these gifts lightly, or cease to wonder at their refreshment, or misuse the power they give to us.

We recognize the awesome responsibility we take upon ourselves when we commit our lives to one another. May we bear that responsibility with honesty and in good faith as well as with joy, and with enough sense of humor to keep us from taking ourselves too seriously.

We bring to you also our fears of love—that we will be asked to give too much, or too little, that when things go wrong—as they will—we may wonder whether we are really right for each other. Help us to put our fears into your hands, in the faith that you will give us resilience for the day when we shall need it. Free us to live our lives together each day in mutual trust, in common concerns, in the gracious sustaining of one another, which is our calling and our great delight. Through Jesus Christ our Lord. Amen.

—Hoyt Hickman

The Sense of a Healing Shadow

My Father, help me to express my willingness to protect without imprisoning, to help without hindering.

I remember when the children were small, and I would go to their beds when they were sick; if they were asleep, I would just lean over and watch, and my shadow would fall across them. I wouldn't touch them because they needed to sleep, and I might awaken them; but I didn't need to touch them. They sensed the protecting shadow, its close but unrestricting presence.

I may not physically cast that shadow over them today, but I pray that through your Spirit it will be there. Let it never darken their enthusiasm, nor restrain their adventure in useful living; but when there is a need, when the forces of illness and evil are preparing to attack, then please, dear Lord, transport that sense of a healing shadow to the sense of battle. In Jesus' name. Amen.

—George W. Erickson

For Home

Father, I pray today for your blessing upon my home:

Here may each member love and be loved.
Here may compassion for others be more important than concern for self.
Here may there be no fear
.to simply say, "I love you."
Here may this love be translated into acts of kindness and words of appreciation.
Here may peace abide and hope abound.
Here may the roots of bitterness vanish and the seeds of benevolence bear fruit.
Here may joy run rampant and patience be practiced.
Here may faith foster faith
from generation to generation.
Here may Christ abide until the earth's a home and all God's children are one. Amen.

—Ronald Patterson

For Sensitivity

Lord, I commit my dear ones to your care today.

I cannot do all that needs to be done for them.

You know their hearts and your plan for their lives.

It is so easy for me to turn them off in the confusion and haste of living. Teach me to sense the unspoken words behind their careless expressions and strange actions.

Help me to really hear their arguments when we differ.

Help them to feel the need for your guidance in the day's tasks. Strengthen them against temptation.

May your Holy Spirit empower me to do my very best in each relationship encountered along my way. Save me from seeking more involvement than I can handle well.

You have taught us to leave the results to you. So, Lord, I will take you at your word and live this day in faithful trust. Amen.

—Mary Ann Hunt

Thanks for Motherhood

Dear Lord, I thank and praise your holy name for giving me the wonderful privilege of being called "Mother." There is such beauty and peace in the sound of that word. Through motherhood, a portion of your wonderful and complete love can be revealed.

Please forgive me when I become irritable about hearing the word "Mother" used so often by my children. It is during these times that I have turned my very being away from your love, and have shut myself off from theirs. Lord, fill me with your Holy Spirit, and use me as an instrument through which my children can see and understand more of you. Amen.

—Jeanie Collier

Prayer for My Family

Father, thank you for a dear and faithful husband. Give him the wisdom he needs to perform his work properly and an expression of love as he relates to his clients and associates.

Be with each member of our family. Thank you for their faith. Keep it ever strong, and give them the inspiration they need to let you continue to mold and change them, that they might be fruitful for you.

Give each one of us today, Lord, a warm heart towards you. Make our minds alert and sensitive toward your Spirit, that we might each be an instrument for your use in every situation confronting us this day. In our Savior's name. Amen.

—Marion Millett

A Home Filled With Love

Our Father,
As we gather under this roof,
sharing the events and feelings of the day,
we give you thanks for our home.
The warmth and coolness,
the order and color of the furnishings,
the taste of good food,
the feel of clean clothes—
all reinforce spoken words of love and discipline.

Thoughts of others who have no house,
or whose family is not really a family,
press in upon us—
sometimes disturbing our sense of well-being.
Free us from crippling feelings of guilt.
Replace them with the kind of love
for you and for them
that gives added meaning and purpose to life.

Show us how to be bridges
between their lives and you—
how to share this home.

We pray in the name of Jesus
who came to open the way
into one family.
Amen.

—Sara B. Harrison

Responsibility of Parenthood

Lord, I feel the responsibility of being a parent.
Give me praise and thanksgiving
for these children (child) of yours and mine!
Give me your vision that I might find hope
in the midst of frustration.
Give me your vision that I might find peace
in the midst of pain.
Give me your vision that I might find love
that accepts the unlovable.
Give me your vision that I might find joy
as I suffer with them.
And forgive me for not letting you
direct my life and theirs more completely.
Amen.

—Betty Yarbrough

A Father's Prayer

Father,

As a father of three children, I thank you for my dear wife, who brought them into being. Her love of you, blended with my love, has been beautiful and meaningful. Her tender, continuing care through joy and sorrow emanated from her authentic commitment to you. Again, I say "Thanks."

For the joys which came into our family experiences—moments of meditation around the breakfast table, picnics with friends, vacation days at church assembly grounds, receiving gifts of substance and encouragement, learning to use and give our talents for others, the sharing of daily decisions—for all of these please accept my gratitude.

For the insights and discoveries which we made as a family, especially in hours of suffering, illness, misunderstanding or failure, we glance backwards and see your guiding hand in all of them. Grant unto us, each in our own way, a fresh confidence that your grace is always available and entirely adequate.

In Jesus' name I pray. Amen.

—Wilson O. Weldon

A Friend to Children

My child needed me today, Lord,
but he didn't get much of my attention.
Where did I fail?
Maybe that's why, at times, I feel
the burden of children.

In some masterful, egocentric way
I'm trying to absorb them into myself
instead of seeing them as
separate,
individual,
creations of God.

You know how it is with my friends.
I can hold them as far off

or as close as they need to be.
I can allow them to fail
since their failure is no reflection on me.
I can allow them to have their growing pains because
I can be objective and
see a positive end.

Yes, I'm relaxed with my friends
for I can see you working your plan.
But, Lord, when I feel as a "parent"
my view gets smogged up.
I need help in feeling like a "friend"
to my children.
Amen.

—Gwen Metzger

A Mother's Prayer

Thank you, God, for the joy, the love, and the happiness my children have brought into my life.

It's so beautiful and thrilling to look into their smiling faces. I just feel so loved even though words often are not even spoken. Then when I hold them tight and they cuddle in my arms, I feel so good all over and can't help saying again and again, "Thank you, God, for such wonderful gifts of love."

When I see them run and play so full of energy and life, I want to tell you again, God, how thankful I am for your blessings.

O God, help me to be more worthy of such love and joy. Help me to be free and ready to share with others.

I want to give my children back to you, God, and simply ask you to guide me as I try to direct them into becoming loving, caring, thoughtful children. Amen.

—Velma Bradley

CHAPTER 6

Personal Prayers

A Personal Prayer

Heavenly Father, please forgive me for not doing the things I should do and for doing those things which I shouldn't do. I am weak and totally dependent on you and your saving grace. I thank you for all the many blessings that you continue to bestow upon me, and the tolerance you have for a sinner such as I.

I thank you for my Christian friends and their understanding and acceptance of me as I am. I thank you for my church and for a dedicated, God-fearing minister who loves you and proclaims the Good News.

Help me when I am weak and in the valley. Please help me not to go down in a vacuum. And, God, thank you for sending your Son, our Savior and Redeemer who died that we might live. I love your Son Jesus with all my heart, soul, and might. Glory hallelujah! Keep me in total peace, and free in spirit, that I might always be a true son of yours and a witness of your love and mercy to all mankind. Amen.

—Thomas Shipmon

I Need You

Father,
I need your love more than ever now.
I need your love . . .
I need the security and confidence
that seems so real from you.
I need you.
I need love
so I can have hope, faith, and assurance
for a safe tomorrow.

The monsters of loneliness
and discouragement
are crushing down upon me.

Because your love can control my life
I need you.
I need the love in your smile
and the love in your touch.
I need you
because you mean so much to me.
Amen.

—Kathie Bell

A Sense of Mission

Lord, you've changed my whole life completely.
In fact, you've changed it so much
that now I sometimes act indiscreetly.
The things that used to be important to me
have exchanged places with my need to *be!*
I find it difficult to spend my day
washing dishes or scrubbing the floor,
when I know there is so much more.
I find it difficult to weed the beds
and cut the grass,
but this is necessary for your beauty to last.
I find it difficult to wash and iron,
to sew and mend,
yet, these two, must be accomplished
again and again.
I'd much rather settle down in the quiet of my room,
with the Scriptures and some books—and not that
  broom!
So help me, Lord, to find a new dimension
of your presence every day. Amen.

                              —Betty Yarbrough

In Silence

Dear Lord, I don't know why I so often ask things of you before I am in tune with your Spirit. So, for a little while, I want to be still and listen to you speak to my heart.

As I listen in quietness, clear my mind . . . relax my body . . . and quicken my spirit.

Bring to my mind the things you would have me discover about myself, the persons I may help or encourage, or the job that only I can do in your name. In silence I wait for you. . . .

—Pat Stubbs

Jesus Comes Today

Lord:

You come to us in strange ways. You've been understood by artists and holy men; you've been praised by saints and sinners alike; you come to us in spectacular films directed by some of Hollywood's most gifted men.

Your joy comes in the first cry of the newborn; and sometimes you dance to the beat of the straining organ. You speak to us through the Phillips' Translation, Good News for Modern Man, and even the King James Version. You've been seen through the church's liturgy and Bible study groups. Your name has been praised through stained-glass windows and bumper stickers.

I saw you in the face of the elderly couple having car trouble. I talked with you when you asked me for some money—to eat your first meal in three days. I saw you in the smile of the accountant who handles student loans. I hear you in some of the latest hit songs.

You come to us everyday, Lord. Open our eyes and ears that we might not miss your coming. Amen.

—Barry McCarty

For Self
Lord, I don't like myself today.
Nothing is going the way I planned.
My hair is a mess.
My personality leaves a lot to be desired.

But somehow I can't help remembering
the time I worked so hard
on that beautiful picture puzzle.
I worked for an hour
trying to get that corner done.
Then I found that crazy piece under the chair.
It certainly was an important part,
wasn't it?
Yet no one piece is more important
than any other.
I needed them all to finish the work.

Yes, I'm beginning to get the message, Lord.
My ragged edges, straight pieces,
and imperfect parts
are all necessary to make "my" part
of the puzzle.
Thank you, Lord, for the shape I take.
I trust you to fit me into
your will and worldwide picture.
Amen.

—Gwen Metzger

Christ's Ambassador

Father,
Being wife, mother, grandmother,
friend, teacher, and confidant
opens many opportunities
to be your ambassador.

As I turn relationships into missions for you,
how freeing it is to know you are responsible
when I follow your Spirit.
You even correct my foolish errors when I run ahead,
or drag behind,
or drift off into some easier byway.

Now I am off to visit a self-pitying old woman.
Lord, I don't really want to go.
It reminds me that I will be old some day—
and I don't like to think about it.

Help me just to share you
and rest in the confidence
that the narrower and darker the place,
the brighter and clearer your light can shine.
Then perhaps you can use me to lift the gloom.
Thank you that Jesus promised to go with us,
even unto the end.
I pray in his name.
Amen.

—Sara B. Harrison

Opportunities to Serve

My Father, I want to do such great things for you that I chafe under the routine of my days. Forgive me for this restlessness. You have blessed me with a loving husband, children, and home. It is these blessings that are my opportunities to serve you.

Help me, I pray, to serve you in doing what is at hand—to be a loving help-mate to my husband, to make our home a living praise to you. And although my children are away and on their own, dear Father, they still need my prayers. May I realize that prayer is a work I can do for you and for them.

Help me, I pray, to be sensitive to the needs of those who come my way and to let you answer them through me. May I yield my restlessness and be content with the way you choose to use me. In Jesus' name. Amen.

—Martha Betts

I Searched for God

Hey God,

I have searched for you so long and needed you so badly. I have searched for you in the noise of everyday life—in the continuous march of humanity, and I have not found you. I have searched for you in the quietness of your places of worship and have not always found you there either.

I have been empty and I have hated some of your children. . . . Now I have found you through your Son, Jesus Christ. Now all the coldness has been made warm; now all the hatred has turned to love. I know you are real because you live inside me and you direct my life. Now through faith I can see your face, I can feel your love and share it with your children, my brothers and sisters.

I feel like running to the top of the highest mountain, and crying out from the depths of my being, "Hey World, it's great to be alive! It's great to love! It's great to be really free!" O Lord, my God, now I believe; now I love; now I live.

—Mark Eugene Fentress

No More Cop-Outs

Lord,
For hours I've been aware
of our frantic search for something
that would allow us to place
this problem back in the box;
to close the lid and pile upon it
stacks of tasks
and other concerns
as we have done before.
The pattern here is well rehearsed
and fortified with custom—
you and me agreeing
to a mutually satisfactory
cop-out.

We've asked for your help before, Father, but here
we are trying to avoid what we so obviously must
face. Help us to understand that loving must sometimes be painful. Bring us to the understanding
that we will never again face anything alone; that
you stand beside us always. Give us the kind of love
that gives and keeps on giving. Amen.

—Marla Visser

Time for God

God, I'm busy. I'm so busy I must confess I forget you too much of the time. It's a shame!

It is not that you skimp on the amount of time you grant to me—a day is a day. To say I'm busy can be an indictment as well as a compliment. It can be a compliment if I really use my time doing worthwhile things. But it can also be an indictment, even if I am working on plans and projects and engaging in activities you can approve. Saying I'm too busy is the same as saying that busyness is my god. This is evil in your sight, for you have said, "You shall have no other god to set against me."

God forgive me. Help me correct myself in the use of the time you give me. Help me each day to think of you frequently, to talk with you often, to ask your advice and help in the constant busyness of my life. Amen.

—Russell Q. Chilcote

CHAPTER 7
Special Prayers

Surprises of Nature

Heavenly Father, we thank you for being the kind of Father who loves us enough to send glad surprises like silent snow in the night to greet us with a morning wonderland; purple and yellow crocuses that peep up through dead earth to thrill our hearts with hope of spring; the dazzling beauty of a cardinal among the pure white blossoms of a dogwood tree! These, O Father, and other lovely tokens of your love help us to know the kind of wonderful friend you are if we will but recognize you in all things beautiful and good.

May we, thus knowing you, respond by doing what will make you happy—by doing good unto the least of your creations. We would have this kind of love for you, our gracious heavenly Father. Amen.

—Mrs. Bachman G. Hodge

Prayer at the End of Summer

Dear God, we come to you with a lot of things on our minds. The summer seems to have gone so quickly. There were things we planned to do, people we planned to see, books we hoped to read, work outdoors we wanted to get done . . . and we didn't.

There were other things we hoped to do, and we did them—places we planned to go, people we hoped to see, and many other special things. The gifts and adventures and sorrows of the summer are in our minds as we come to you.

But we are glad that summer's over, too.

We wonder about the year that lies ahead: What will school be like this year? What will happen on our block and in our home and around the world? And will our dreams for this year come true?

Help us to use this new beginning well. And as we enter the season of activity again, let us not be overburdened with our work, or assume too much of the world's anxiety upon ourselves, or be driven by some false need to prove ourselves. For in your love we are already accepted and free!

So help us, trusting in your love and in each other, to do what we can do and be who we can be, through Jesus Christ our Lord. Amen.

—Hoyt Hickman

Worldwide Communion Sunday

Today, Father, Christians around the world will be coming before you in a time of special worship. I thank you that geography is no hindrance to your Spirit. Mountains, rivers, and oceans cannot keep us apart who are together in you.

So, in these quiet moments, I would ask you to sustain me by the presence of my children—far removed by distance and even life-styles—by the presence of my friends and other family members; by the presence of that multitude who are my brothers and sisters in your forever family.

Father, your forgiving love and grace make my heart yearn for those over whom your Spirit yearns. May they receive your sent faith even now to believe and worship you, as do we, while the Spirit of Jesus makes these affirmations and petitions through even us. Amen.

—Sally Gallaway

Thanksgiving Day

O God, on this Thanksgiving Day we are moved to express to thee the thankfulness which fills our hearts. As the Pilgrim Fathers offered their thanksgiving for thy provisions of food, clothes, and home, so do we. As life in a new world proved challenging to those who lived then, so let the world of our time challenge us to use our hands and minds to glorify thee through contributing to the welfare of mankind and thus serving our great country.

As we gather around the family board for our Thanksgiving meal, we are grateful for our family—that we are bound together by our love for thee and for one another. Thou art the God of love. Thou art our Father. Help us to live as thy children. In Jesus' name. Amen.

—William P. Anderson, Jr.

Christmas

O thou Christ of Christmas, hear our prayer. On this day of days we praise thee and we worship thee. With the millions of all lands we give thanks to thee for thy great glory.

For the angels' message to the shepherds we thank thee; for the good tidings of great joy—that God cares, that he purposes to make a better world, a kindlier world, to give the gospel to the poor, to heal the brokenhearted, to deliver the captives, to recover sight to the blind, to set free the oppressed.

O thou Christ of Christmas, help us to block no longer this coming of thy kingdom. Help us to share thy great unselfishness—thy passion for the world—for men of every nation, creed, and color, for the poor and neglected, the burdened and oppressed. May the Spirit of Christmas find a way into our hearts, helping us to exclaim, "Joy to the world! the Lord is come!" Amen.

—Ralph S. Cushman

New Year's Day
Lord, I know that New Year's Day
is a time of new beginnings
           of resolutions
           of proposals
           and challenges.
As I face this new year,
may I see each day as the dawning of new life,
given as the gift of God's love,
and received in joyful celebration.

Help me in this daily celebration:
           to begin each day as if it were the last,
           to accept your forgiveness of all that's past,
           to respond to your presence within,
           to reach out in your compassion to others.

Be my Alpha and Omega each day, Lord.
Resurrect me in your power
to live your way
in joyful obedience.
                Amen.

                      —Betty Yarbrough

Growth and Change

When you and I were young
our love was willow-green with summer;
supple, lush, its branches danced in every breeze,
laughed and cried in turn, each lightly, carelessly.
We smiled to ourselves and fancied our love to be
straight, strong, beautiful oak, the envy of all.
Then the winter came, our limbs grew brittle,
winds howled, whipped and tore till all around us
was littered with the branches of our dreams.
We grew, we learned, we changed,
until our summer willow fantasies emerged
as oak; not straight and tall,
but gnarled, twisted mountain oak,
its roots firmly planted in the bedrock of our
faith in God, determined and free,
proud of its survival; its branches bent
to the needs of each other,
not to pleasing another's eye,
leafy-green with new love dreams,
reaching for the stars.

Lead us to understand, God, that living in love
is living in a life of growth and change. Help us to
realize that when we try to stay the same, we become stagnant and dead. Help us to accept all the
beautiful changes in our lives as gifts from you.
Amen.

—Marla Visser

A Prisoner's Prayer

All Mighty Father, I come to you in Jesus' name. I have come because I am tired and discouraged and I am looking for something better in life, and I need to know that somebody cares. I am not ashamed to worship God. I have come to let the world know that I believe in God.

O Lord, I confess before you and my fellowman that I have failed myself and others because I have been unwilling to change, because I was afraid to really look at myself.

I ask that you will grant me mercy for the way I've treated others, and give me a chance to start again to make my life worthwhile. Through the life and death of Jesus Christ, who taught us how to live and how to die, God has promised new life. I am loved. I am accepted, I have been forgiven.

I may be treated like a nobody, or even act like a nobody; I may be poor and on my own, without friends; I may get discouraged and frustrated here in prison; but no matter what happens to me, Lord, help me always to remember that I am worthwhile in your eyes, that I am somebody in Christ Jesus. Amen.

—Robert A. Johnson

Prayer of a Working Mother

Father, sometimes I am frustrated and confused by the opposition to mothers working. But it seems that you have always been with me, assuring me that it was right, and opening the right doors at just the right time.

Thank you, Father, for giving us the right ingredients in our home to make my working "workable." You've provided a husband and children who are both loving and understanding. We have learned to work together and share responsibility and in doing this we've grown closer to each other. We have found that each of us has an important part to contribute to this family.

I need to pray for your help continually as I carry out the task of working and trying to be a wife and mother at the same time.

Father, quiet my frustrations and anxieties. Give me the organization that I need to carry out the tasks you've given me. Continue to guide my path, dear Lord, and give me the wisdom to follow that guidance. Amen.

—Mary Ann Clinard

Easter Morning

Our Father, on this Easter day we are thankful anew that thou hast set the solitary in families. We thank thee for families, for our family, and for thy promises that we need not be solitary or lonely if thou art with us.

We rejoice today because of the Easter fact. We thank thee because of what the resurrection means to us, to so many families, to the church, and to the world.

We thank thee for the Easter message, its word of hope and its promise of immortality. We rejoice that the tomb was empty; and because he lives we, too, shall live. Strengthen our belief in the living Christ, who, on that first Easter morn long ago, came forth triumphant from the tomb. May the triumphant Christ abide with each of us here today and with those of our family who are far away. May he also reign in the hearts of thy people everywhere. In the name of the risen Christ. Amen.

—J. Manning Potts

Wedding Day

Author of all love, we ask thy blessing on our dear one who is to be married today. As we have shared our love for one another over the years, so now help us to extend our love to this new member of our family circle.

Grant that these two shall realize fully that marriage is an eternal union. Let them see their lives as blended into one harmony, that together they may share all things, bear all things, enjoy all things, achieve all things.

Let thy blessings be on the home they are establishing, that it may bless all who live in it and shed a mantle of light on the whole community. May they so live together the life that now is, that in the world to come they may have life everlasting. In Jesus' name. Amen.

—T. Cecil Myers

Those on the Highways
Lord,
be with those who drive our highways for a living.
Guide the patrolmen and truck drivers
who know the monotony of white and yellow lines,
and the loneliness of mileage signs.
Help them to know that we depend on them
for highway assistance and economic survival.
Be with them when the glamor of road life
and the freedom of travel
turns into the fight of fatigue
and the dangers of drowsiness.
Be with them—and with us—as we travel
these same highways together.
In Jesus' name.
Amen.

—Barry McCarty

Birth of a Child

Dear Lord, whose Son Jesus was once a baby, bless our baby that he (she) may grow as thy Son grew—in wisdom and stature, and in favor with God and man. May he (she) be a joy to his (her) parents and of service to the world. As parents, we thank thee, O Creator God, that thou has blessed us in sharing thy creative activity, bringing new life into being through an expression of love. Glory be to thee for the miracle of birth and for the marvel of love. Through Christ, thy Son, our Lord. Amen.

—Fred R. Stair, Jr.

Dedication of a Home

Heavenly Father, we ask your blessing on this house—its strong walls, its sturdy roof, its firm foundation. May its rafters ring with glad songs and laughter. May its walls encompass those who live within and protect them from storm and wind, from snow and rain, and heat of summer sun. Help us to make it a temple of your love, a home of Christian truth and worship. Let all who enter it feel the warmth of our fellowship and know that you are the foundation of our home. Amen.

—Lois M. Ames

For Daddy Away on Business

Dear God, our Daddy is away. Even when he is not here, we love him, and we know he loves us and is working to help us.

Because our family loves each other no matter how far apart we are, we know your love can be with us everywhere all of the time. Thank you, God, for love.

We thank you for taking care of us and for taking care of Daddy. Help us to help Mother while he is gone and to be good cooperators. We thank you for all the cooks and hotel people who help make Daddy comfortable away from home and for the train men and airplane people who bring him back to us safely.

Help all families everywhere to live together in peace and happiness. Amen.

—The William Genné Family

Prayer for Mother Away From Home

Dear God,

It is so comforting to know that we have a heavenly Father who cares for each member of the family as we are far apart this day. Uphold each member of my family with the strength which comes from thee. Help them to have patience and understanding, and perhaps to even go out of their way to show a special kindness to each other while I am gone.

O God, may we remember that as we are away from each other that each is an *ambassador* representing our family. May we stay true to the convictions that we have worked through together as a family.

When I arrive home, may I be a better mother to the children and a more loving, caring wife to my husband as I seek to tend to each one's needs. Now, may the Lord watch between us in a special way as we are absent one from the other. In Jesus' name. Amen.

—Lois O. Schwob

CHAPTER 8

Prayers for the World

For the Whole Wide World

Dear Lord, we thank thee that thou dost love to have us talk with thee.

We need to pray for our big, big world today.

We pray that we may see what we can do for the world in its fear and agony and hate.

We pray for our President, our Secretary of State, and our Congress.

We cannot pray for the power to destroy or defeat another country with arms; but we do pray that love may take the place of hate, and faith may take the place of fear in our relations with differing governments.

We ask thee to guide us as we start in a new direction, in the direction of helping the desperate underprivileged people of the world out of their misery and frustration.

May America and her allies vie with others in a tremendous effort to raise the entire world up

to a level of happiness and prosperity and hope.
We pray that the churches, business, philanthropy,
and the government may unite in an all-out,
nation-wide War of Amazing Kindness to the
world.
We have talked and prayed and sung and believed
so much bigger than we have acted in the past.
Help us from this time on to match our words with
our works.
Send down thy love upon all mankind in such a
tremendous river that this world of strife can be
transformed into the kingdom of love.
With this prayer we offer ourselves. In Jesus' name.
Amen.

—Frank C. Laubach

For Heaven's Blessings

I pray heaven to bestow the best of blessings on
this house and on all that shall hereafter inhabit it.
May none but honest and wise men ever rule under
this roof.

—John Adams
Sixth President of the United States

**This prayer is carved over the fireplace of the State Dining
Room in the White House.**

Who Is My Neighbor?

O Lord,
who is my neighbor?
My neighbor enjoys the freedom of expression
                    and the rights of liberty
                        and justice for all.
        But too often he lies in the gutter,
                            dirty,
                            sick,
                and starving. . . .
My neighbor has that great feeling that he "belongs"
            to a group
            to someone—and enjoys the thrill
            of just being alive.
But too often he sits at home
    or walks the streets alone,
    afraid and uncertain. . . .
My neighbor is "free, white, and twenty-one."
            But my neighbor is also black,
            and chained by superstition
            and hatred. . . .
Help me, O Lord,
to see people as persons
and to love my neighbor
as myself.
In your name, I pray.
Amen.

—Ronald Patterson

Lord of Space

Dear God and Father of all mankind:

In this dread hour when man hurls satellites to circle the earth, when he multiplies missiles and atomic warheads, when he seals himself into cylinders and explores the moon, we pray the prayer of our forefathers:

"Lord God of hosts, be with us yet,
Lest we forget—lest we forget!"

Lest we forget that thou still art Lord of space and Master of time.

Lest we forget that thine ancient laws and thine eternal verities still stand, outwearing time and circumstance.

Lest we forget, in this hour of mingled hopes and fears, that thou art from everlasting to everlasting, unshaken and secure.

Lord God, of hosts, of atoms and of satellites, be with us yet, lest we forget. Amen.

—Lawrence E. Nelson

God Bless All the People
God, bless all the people in the world.
Wait a minute that means everybody, doesn't it?
It means
All my foes.
Lord, don't bless all the people in the world.
Wait a minute that isn't right either.
Love thy neighbor.
What'd you say, Lord?
Love thy neighbor.
Surely, Lord, you don't mean that.
They hate me next door, Lord.
They're mean. . . .
But, Lord, they're different, think different,
look different.
Judge not that they be not judged.
Well. . . .
I suppose nobody's perfect.
But nobody's totally imperfect either.
Hey, maybe you're right there.
Lord, bless all the people in the world.
Amen.

—David Randolph, III

Neighbors Around the World

Dear Lord, we thank you for neighbors.

We thank you for the friendship and devotion that real neighbors have for one another. We also thank you for the many blessings that we have received from our neighbors.

O Master, keep us mindful of the great need for neighborly love among untold millions across the world. By your perfect love, multiply our concern, our caring, our love. Then use our love, Lord; send it out to lonely ones who need to feel your presence, and who crave the assurance that neighbors somewhere are caring for them.

We want to feel that all those you love are our neighbors, wherever they are. Bless them, Master, in your dear name. Amen.

—Gail and Dorcas Kurtz

For World Brotherhood

Our Father, we come to you to bring our adoration and our thanks that we can call you Father. We know that in calling you Father we accept as brothers all men of all nations who bow to you. We know that in your Kingdom there is no first- or second-rate citizenship based on color or creed.

We pray for tolerance and understanding. We know in our hearts that we should be able to accept all men as equals, but in our minds we allow social pressures to cause us to rationalize. We allow blind prejudice to color our attitudes and affect our actions. Forgive us, we pray.

Give us, O God, wisdom and courage—wisdom to know what your will is in each situation and courage to stand for that which you reveal to us.

Help us, we pray. Amen.

—H. Eugene Smith

CHAPTER 9

Morning and Evening Prayers

When Work Is Laid Aside

Our heavenly Father, after our daily work is laid aside and we gather together in this loving circle for prayer, we feel a refreshing sense of peace and happiness in thy presence. Here in the affection of our family all blessings are enriched, all cares shared, all sorrows softened.

In the turmoil of daily striving, forbid that we yield to selfish ease and mean ambitions. Strengthen our spirits, enlighten our minds, and elevate our desires that we may devote our energies to thy service. May we live together in love and unselfishness so that happiness and contentment may abide within our home. Amen.

—Edwin R. Hartz

Before I Sleep

O God, before I sleep tonight, I must turn my family back to your care in a very special way. Today our last daughter left for college, and our home is very quiet indeed.

As I miss the security of talking with each one each day, there is joy in knowing that we all talk to you. As I miss their companionship, I am sure of your abiding closeness to each of us.

I pray, O Father, that each one will wake tomorrow with joy. May they know the excitement and happiness and fulfillment of your world. May their minds and their hearts and their souls be stretched as they are exposed to new places, new people, new ideas.

I feel emptied and limp tonight, but I shall sleep well, having confidence in my children and great trust in you.

Help us now, to keep close to each other and to you. In Jesus' name I pray. Amen.

—Mamie Lee Finger

A Morning Prayer
Good morning, God!
We're glad you're here
because we need somebody to talk to about our
joy as a family.
As a matter of fact, we consider you
a member of our family.
Come to think of it, we're members of
your family too!

We're glad we are a family.
It's great to be able to go to sleep at night
knowing that we're with persons we love.
We feel secure because we know that
we are loved by every other person
in our home.
We are especially glad that you love us all!

Each of us has a special joy and we want to
share our joy with everyone in the family:
(*Here, let each person share his or her particular
reason for gladness*).
How about you, God?
Do you have a bit of joy that you can share with us
this morning?
(Here, let everyone reflect quietly for a moment;

perhaps God will speak.)
We are excited about this new day, God.
Each of us has a plan for the day and we want to
share that plan with everyone in the family:
(*Here, let each person share*
his or her plan for the day).

It occurs to us that
you've given us this new day, God.
Perhaps you have a plan for our day.
Tell us if you have something special
for us to do today?
(*Here, let everyone reflect quietly for a moment;*
perhaps a new task will emerge.)

It's time now to get busy with our tasks.
We want to help each other reach our goals.
Will you guide us?
If our goal is a wrong one
or if we seek to reach our goal
through insensitive and unkind means,
please correct us!

Thank you for this time together, God.
We're glad you're a part of our
family.
Amen.

—Harold Bales

Prayer for Today

Dear God above, I give you thanks for a new day. This is your day. May I use it well and unto your liking.

The way ahead, Father, often seems uncertain. At these times keep me in remembrance that you have promised that all will be well. I need your support and courage.

May your Spirit remain with me throughout this day and may I be sensitive to your guidance. I need the help of your vision and leadership. O Lord above all, may I be understanding of other's needs, also. I pray that others might come with me in the constant bond of your love and compassion.

I ask forgiveness for my many sins and shortcomings, through Jesus Christ your son. Amen.

—Fleeta Davis

A New Day!

Lord, thank you for the new day that is rapidly approaching. Grant me wisdom to use it wisely. Help me to show compassion and care for all those that I associate with this day. Let me just be myself without any masks or make-believe. Help me to witness to others when I should and grant me the wisdom to keep silent and listen when it is best. Help me to be honest and fair with everyone I deal with today.

Grant me, Father, the opportunity to be a booster —not a knocker; a pusher—not a kicker; a motor —not a clog. Let me impart an air of optimism into the presence of everyone I meet. Help me to expect difficulty, trials, and tribulation; but help me to force my way through them. Thank you for sending your Son who died for my sins that I might live and have life abundantly. I pray in Jesus' name. Amen.

—Thomas Shipmon